Zane
Visiting the Dentist

CHRISTINE REDA

Copyright @2021 by Christine Reda

All rights reserved. No part of this book may be reproduced in any form or by any electronic or mechanical means, including information storage and retrieval systems, without permission in writing from the publisher, except by reviewers, who may quote brief passages in a review.

This publication contains the opinions and ideas of its author. It is intended to provide helpful and informative material on the subjects addressed in the publication. The author and publisher specifically disclaim all responsibility for any liability, loss or risk, personal or otherwise, which is incurred as a consequence, directly or indirectly, of the use and application of any of the contents of this book.

WORKBOOK PRESS LLC
187 E Warm Springs Rd,
Suite B285, Las Vegas, NV 89119, USA

Website: https://workbookpress.com/
Hotline: 1-888-818-4856
Email: admin@workbookpress.com

Ordering Information:
Quantity sales. Special discounts are available on quantity purchases by corporations, associations, and others. For details, contact the publisher at the address above.

ISBN-13: 978-1-954753-50-1 (Paperback Version)
978-1-954753-51-8 (Digital Version)

REV. DATE: 12.03.2021

After writing Zane Visiting the Dentist, Zane will be a good example for his new little sister, Alexia Rose and his cousin that was born earlier this year, Axyl Walker. My hope is that Zane will be a good influence on not only to his little sister and cousin, but to all of my readers as well. Feel free to comment and give feedback and positive thoughts on this book.

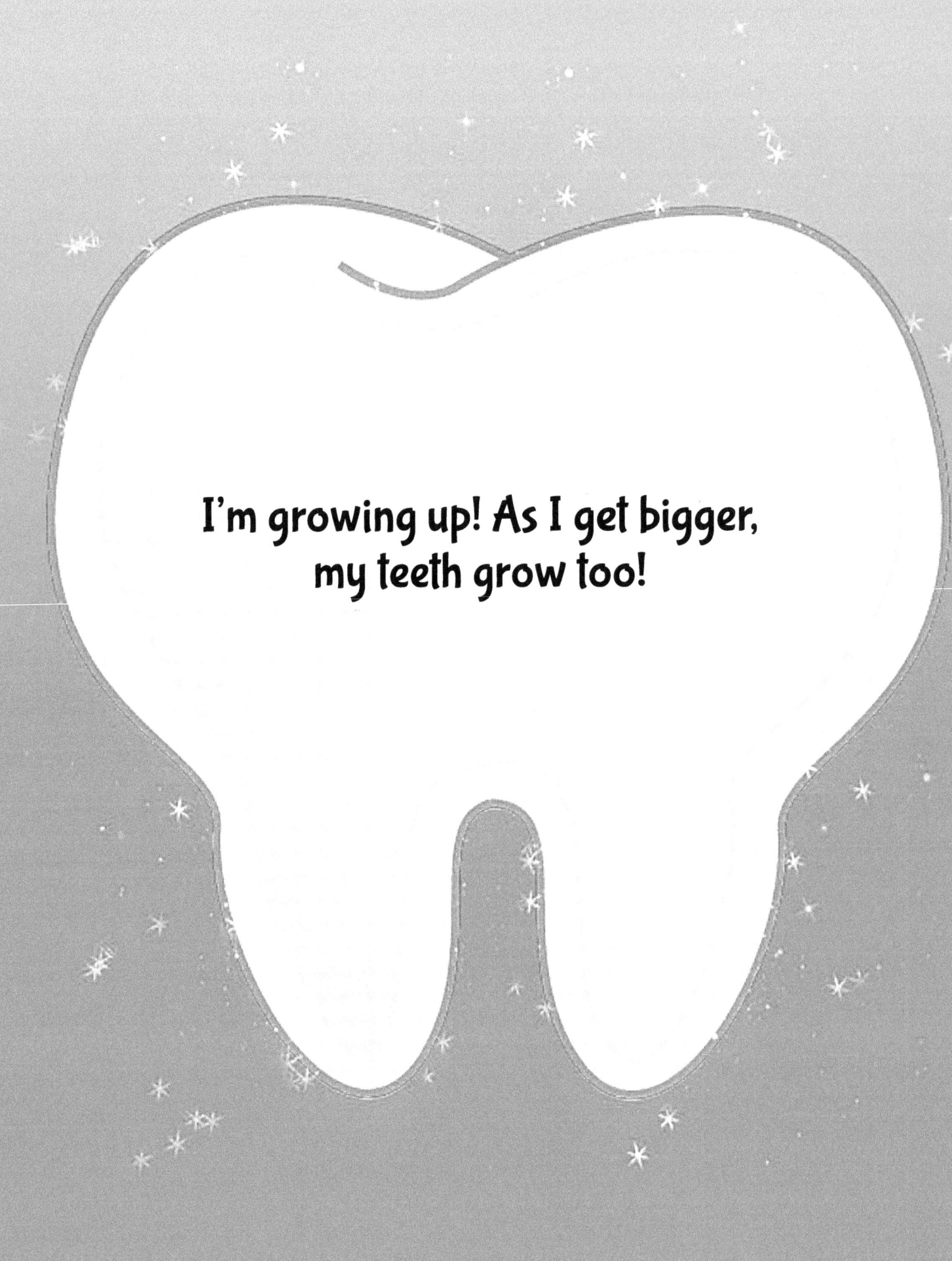

I'm growing up! As I get bigger, my teeth grow too!

When I was a baby, my parents cleaned my gums with a warm wash cloth after I ate or drank. I didn't have any teeth to clean yet. This helped keep my mouth healthy.

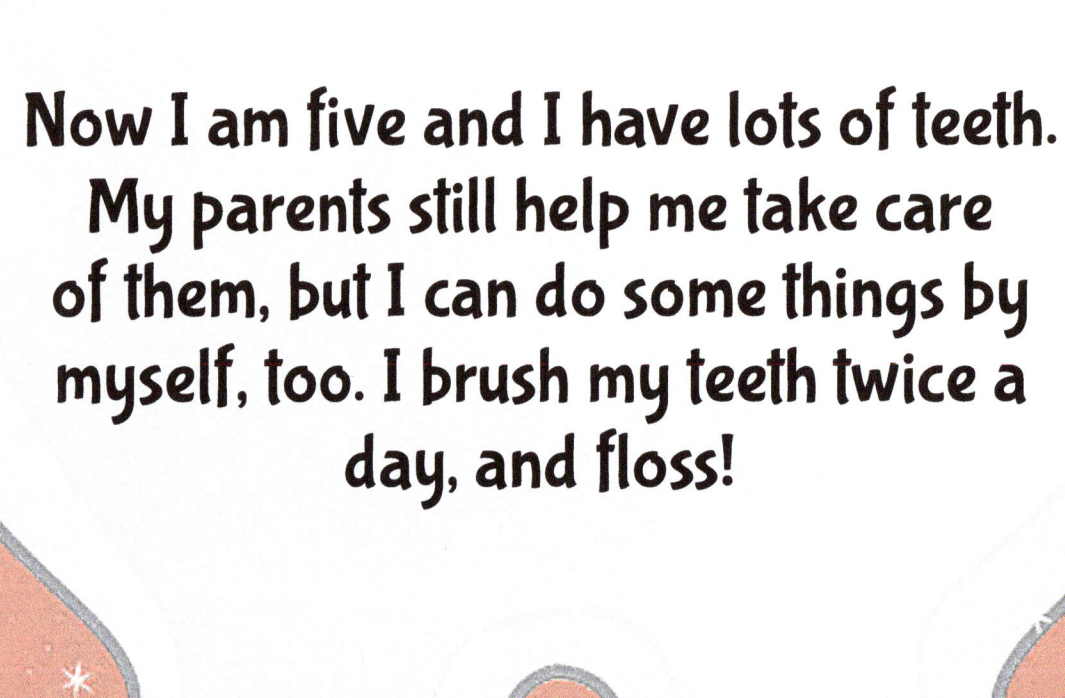

Now I am five and I have lots of teeth. My parents still help me take care of them, but I can do some things by myself, too. I brush my teeth twice a day, and floss!

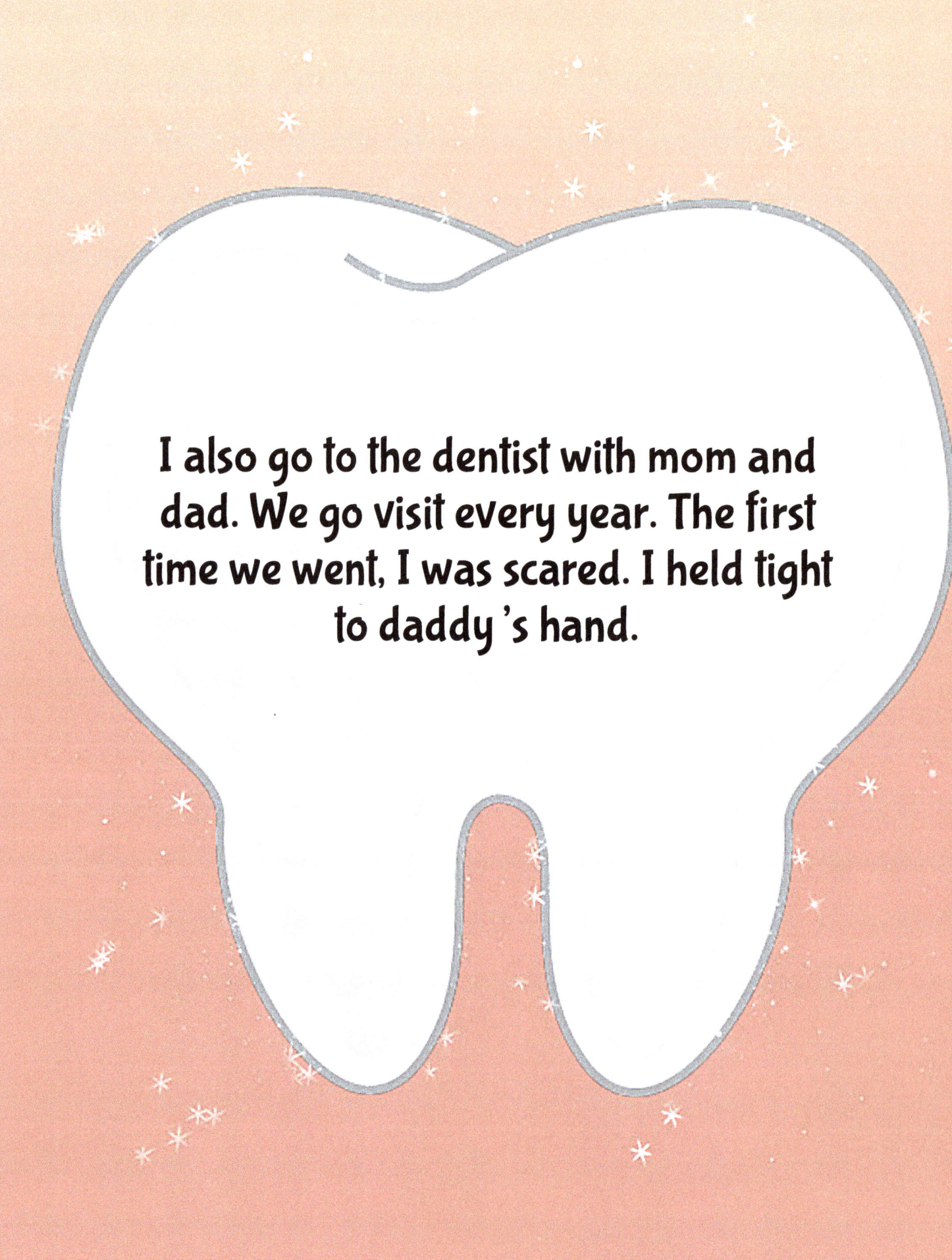

I also go to the dentist with mom and dad. We go visit every year. The first time we went, I was scared. I held tight to daddy's hand.

Daddy told me he would sit by me for the whole visit. He said I could ask the dentist anything I wanted, so I would feel safe.

My favorite part of the dentist is the dentist chair. It can go up and down by itself! Sometimes Dr. Zachary lets me push the button to take it down.

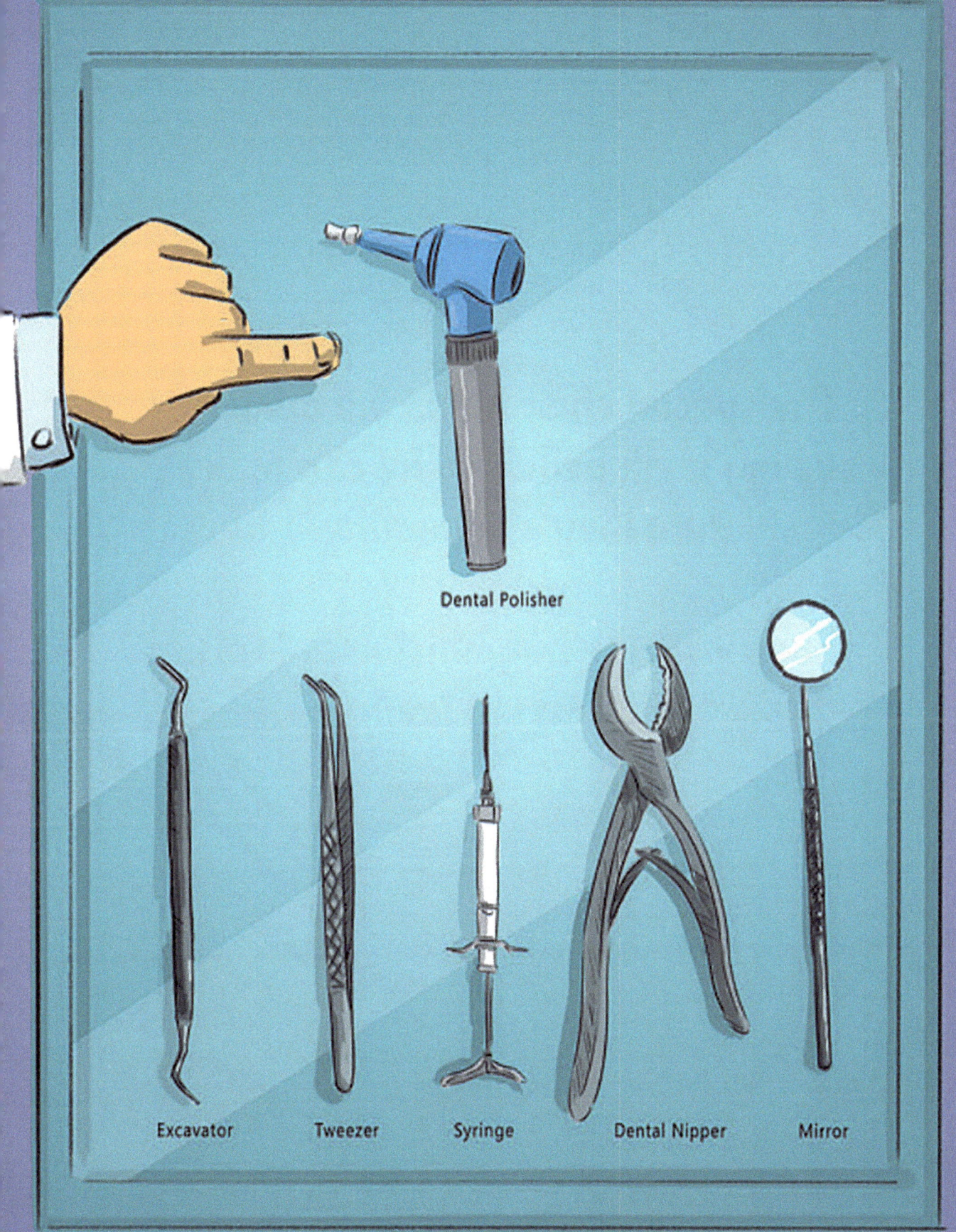

The special chair helps the dentist see my teeth better, so he can make sure they are healthy.

Each visit, the hygienist uses tools to clean my teeth.

Then the dentist gives my mouth a check up, like the doctor. He checks my teeth and gums and he takes an x-ray of my mouth. The x-ray helps the dentist see inside my teeth, like he's seeing through a window. The x-ray shows any cavities that are hiding inside. Cavities make your teeth hurt and make it hard to eat.

Dad says he is proud of me when the dentist tells him I have no new cavities. That means I'm taking good care of my teeth! Dr. Zachary gives me a big high five. Then I get a new toothbrush and some extra-special strawberry flavored toothpaste.

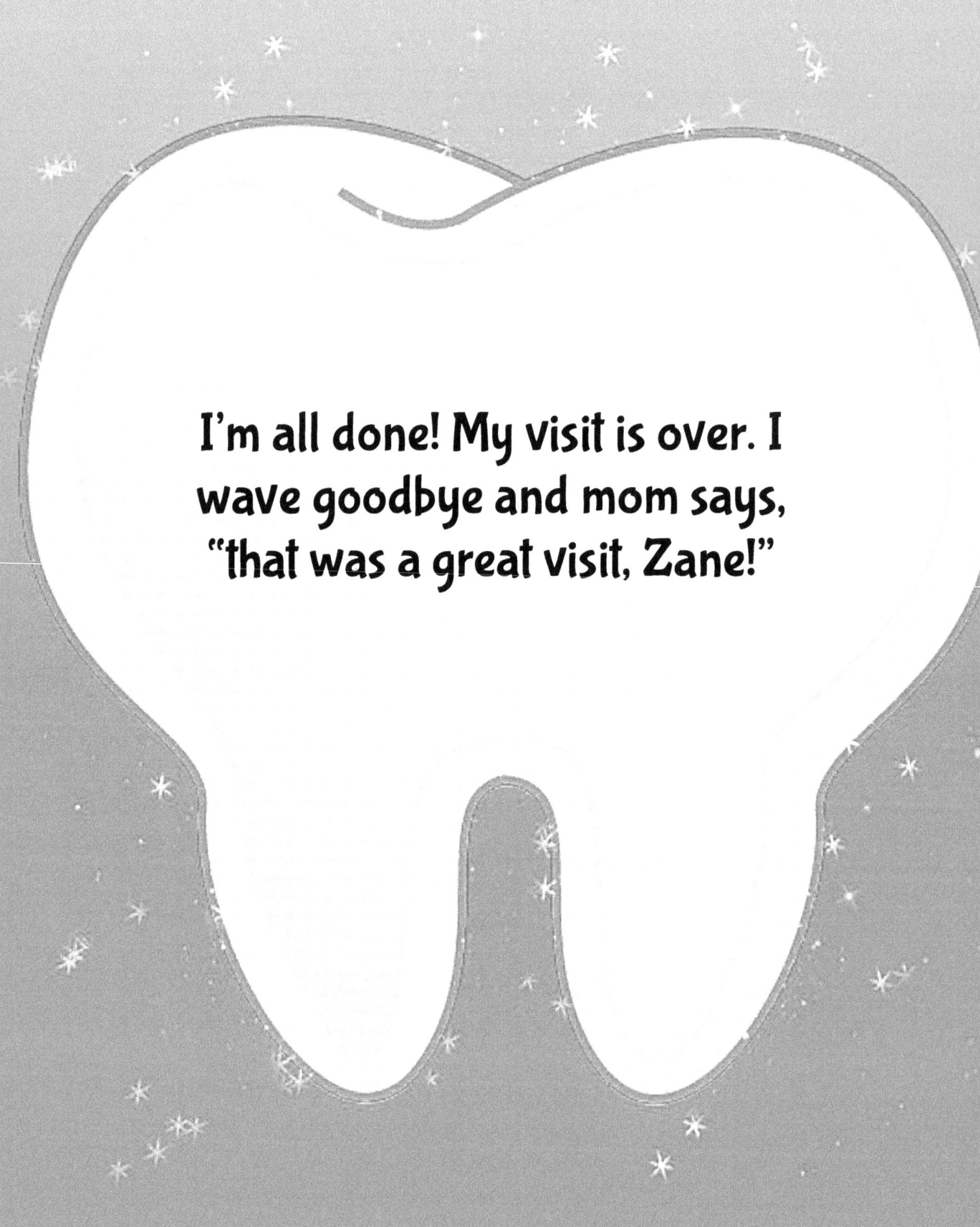

I'm all done! My visit is over. I wave goodbye and mom says, "that was a great visit, Zane!"

www.ingramcontent.com/pod-product-compliance
Lightning Source LLC
Chambersburg PA
CBHW061108070526
44579CB00011B/175